INSTANT SUCCESS

Like-Instrument Starting System
To Complement All Band Methods

Dear Band Student,

Congratulations! You have made one of the most important choices of your life by joining the band. The key to *Instant Success* is your commitment to daily practice. Each time you learn a new note, count a new rhythm or play a song with a friend, you become a more accomplished musician. We are thrilled to welcome you to our band family, and wish you the very best for a lifetime of musical enjoyment.

Tom C. Rhodes   **Donald Bierschenk**   **Tim Lautzenheiser**

Michael Sweeney   **Linda Petersen**

History

of MUSICAL INSTRUMENTS

Musical instruments have been an important part of every culture since pre-historic times. Wood, metal, string and even animal skins have been used to create instruments designed to communicate signals, express feelings and play songs.

Woodwind instruments were refined in the mid-1840's by Theobald Boehm and Adolph Sax, who invented the saxophone. Heinrich Stölzel added valves to trumpets and horns in the early 1800's. String instruments existed in the early Middle Ages (500 - 1430). Percussion and keyboard instruments have roots dating back to 3500 B.C.

The flute, oboe, bassoon, all clarinets and all saxophones are members of the woodwind family. Brass instruments include the trumpet, cornet, horn, trombone, baritone and tuba. Snare drum, bass drum, bells, cymbals, xylophone and tambourine are members of the percussion family. The string family is made up of the violin, viola, violincello, string bass and guitar. The keyboard family includes the piano, harpsichord and computerized keyboard instruments.

Most musical instruments resembled their present appearance by the time World War I began in 1914. Today's manufacturers continue to improve all instruments. Recent developments, such as computers and synthesizers (MIDI) add exciting possibilities to our ever-expanding world of music.

ISBN 0-7935-2476-8

Hal Leonard Publishing Corporation

00862529

7777 West Bluemound Road P.O. Box 13819 Milwaukee, WI 53213

Breathing & Air Stream

Breathing is natural thing we all do constantly. To discover the correct air stream to play your trumpet:

- Place the palm of your hand near your mouth.
- Inhale deeply and keep your shoulders steady. Your waist should expand like a balloon.
- Slowly whisper "tah" as you gradually exhale air into your palm.

The air you feel is the air stream. It produces sound through the instrument. Your tongue is like a faucet or valve in that it releases the air stream.

Producing Your Tone

Tone is musical sound. "Buzzing" through the mouthpiece produces your tone. The buzz is a fast vibration in the center of your lips. Embouchure (*ahm-bah-shure*) is your mouth's position on the mouthpiece of the instrument. A good embouchure takes time and effort, so carefully follow these steps for success:

BUZZING

- Moisten your lips.
- Say the letter "m" to bring your lips together.
- Relax your jaw to separate your upper and lower teeth.
- Form a slightly puckered smile to firm the corners of your mouth.
- Direct a full air stream through the center of your lips, creating a buzz.
- Buzz frequently without your mouthpiece.

MOUTHPIECE PLACEMENT

- Form your "buzzing" embouchure.
- Center the mouthpiece on your lips. Your teacher may suggest a slightly different mouthpiece placement.
- Take a full breath.
- Buzz through the center of your lips. Strive to keep a steady, even buzz.
- Your lips provide a cushion for the mouthpiece.

Mouthpiece Work-Outs

Like a physical work-out, mouthpiece work-outs may make you dizzy and tired at first. Keep practicing, and you'll see daily improvement.

Hold the mouthpiece on the stem with your thumb and first finger. Carefully form your embouchure, take a deep breath and hold still. Strive for a steady, even buzz. Your work-out look like this:

For higher tones, make the opening in the center of your lips more firm. For lower tones, slightly relax the opening.

Getting It Together

Throughout this book, all instructions apply to both cornets and trumpets because they are played exactly the same way.

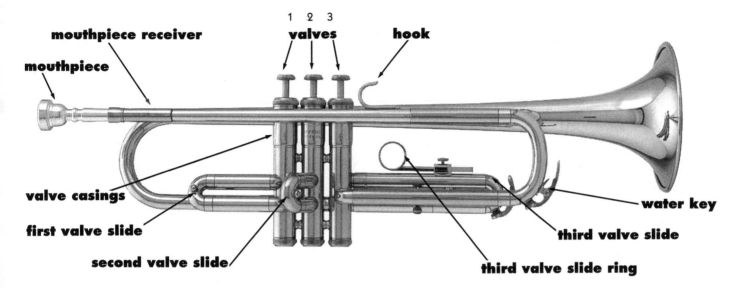

Step 1 - Put your left thumb and fingers around the valve casings and pick up the trumpet. Your left hand supports the weight of the instrument.

Step 1 - Put your left thumb and fingers around the valve casings and pick up the trumpet. Your left hand supports the weight of the instrument.

Step 2 - Place your left ring finger inside the ring of the third valve slide.

Step 3 - Hold the mouthpiece at the wide end with your right hand. Gently twist the mouthpiece into the mouthpiece receiver.

Step 4 - Arch your right hand to form a backwards "C". Place your thumb below the first and second valve casings. Place your little finger on top of the hook.

Step 5 - Always sit or stand tall when playing. Hold the trumpet as shown:

Posture

Sit on the edge of your chair and always keep your:
• Spine straight and tall
• Shoulders back and relaxed
• Feet flat on the floor

Long Tone 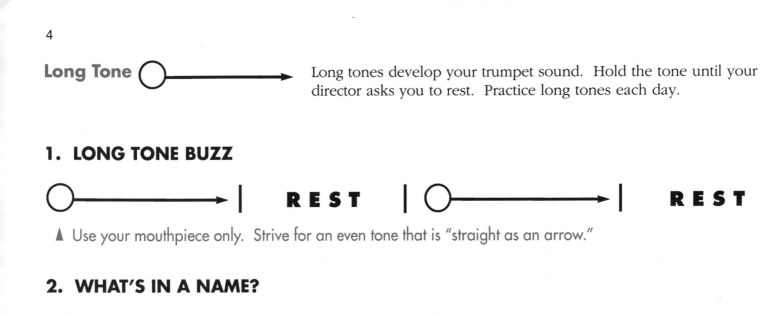 Long tones develop your trumpet sound. Hold the tone until your director asks you to rest. Practice long tones each day.

1. LONG TONE BUZZ

R E S T | R E S T |

▲ Use your mouthpiece only. Strive for an even tone that is "straight as an arrow."

2. WHAT'S IN A NAME?

R E S T | R E S T |

▲ Long tones have names. Your teacher will tell you to write G or C inside the circle, like this: (G)

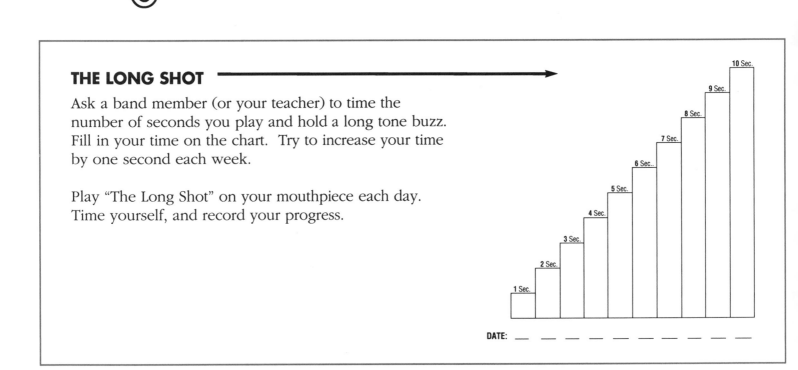

THE LONG SHOT

Ask a band member (or your teacher) to time the number of seconds you play and hold a long tone buzz. Fill in your time on the chart. Try to increase your time by one second each week.

Play "The Long Shot" on your mouthpiece each day. Time yourself, and record your progress.

1 Sec. 2 Sec. 3 Sec. 4 Sec. 5 Sec. 6 Sec. 7 Sec. 8 Sec. 9 Sec. 10 Sec.

DATE: __ __ __ __ __ __ __ __ __ __

3. LET'S PLAY "C"   Carefully assemble your trumpet (see page 3).

C (C) R E S T | (C) R E S T |
○ ○ ○

▲ "C" is played with open valves.

4. PLAY "C" AGAIN

(C) | (C) | R E S T | (C) |

► Take a quick, full breath before playing the second "C".

5. LET'S PLAY "D"

▲ The black circles tell you which valve keys to press down.

6. WHAT A PAIR

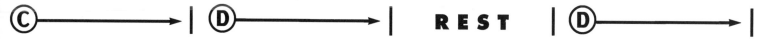

► Play long tones every day on each new tone you learn on your instrument.

7. LET'S PLAY "E"

8. THREE TONES

Go to next line.

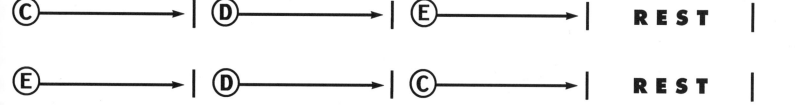

HIGH AND LOW TONES

Music is made with high and low tones. Your teacher will play two tones on an instrument. Listen carefully, and **raise** your hand if the second tone is **higher**. Lower your hand if the second tone is **lower**. You may want to sing the pitches after your teacher plays them.

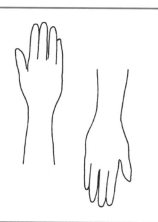

9. INSTANT SUCCESS QUIZ

Your teacher will play two tones on an instrument. Write "H" if the second tone is higher than the first tone. Write an "L" if the second tone is lower than the first tone. Listen carefully.

A. _____   B. _____   C. _____   D. _____   E. _____

READING MUSIC

Symbols, letters and numbers make up the basic instructions for reading music.
Identify and draw each of these symbols:

Music Staff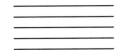

The music staff has
5 lines and 4 spaces.

**Measures
Bar Lines**

Bar lines divide the
music staff into measures.

Notes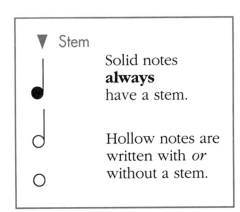

Notes are placed on the music staff and
tell us how **high** or **low** to play.

Different note shapes tell us
how **long** to play tones.

10. PLAY "E" ON THE MUSIC STAFF   Hold each long tone until your teacher asks you to rest.

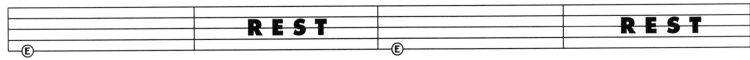

► "E" is placed on the bottom line of the music staff.

11. PLAY "D" ON THE MUSIC STAFF   How many measures are in this exercise?

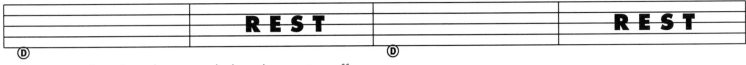

► "D" is placed on the space below the music staff.

12. "E" AND "D" TOGETHER

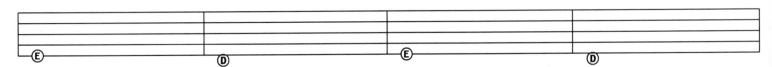

► Be sure to take quick, full breaths between long tones.

Leger Lines

◄ Leger lines

◄ Leger lines

Leger lines extend the music staff. Leger line notes appear above *and* below the music staff.

13. LEGER LINE "C"

-C-   -C-   -C-   -C-

► "C" is placed on the first leger line below the music staff.

Double Bar   A double bar indicates the end of a piece of music.

14. THREE LONG TONES

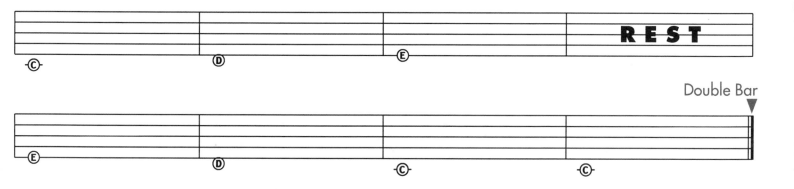

-C-   D   E   **R E S T**

Double Bar

E   D   -C-   -C-

Beat   The **beat** is the **pulse** of music. Find your pulse by placing two fingertips on your wrist below your thumb. Your heart **beats** to create your **pulse**.

The beat in music is very steady, just like your pulse. The beat must remain **very even** when you practice alone, or with other band members. Counting aloud and foot-tapping help us follow a steady beat.

Tap your foot **down** on the number and **up** on the "&". One beat = **1 &.**
↓ ↑

15. COUNT AND TAP THE BEAT

Count	1	&	2	&	3	&	4	&	1	&	2	&	3	&	4	&	1	&	2	&	3	&	4	&	1	&	2	&	3	&	4	&
Tap	↓	↑	↓	↑	↓	↑	↓	↑	↓	↑	↓	↑	↓	↑	↓	↑	↓	↑	↓	↑	↓	↑	↓	↑	↓	↑	↓	↑	↓	↑	↓	↑

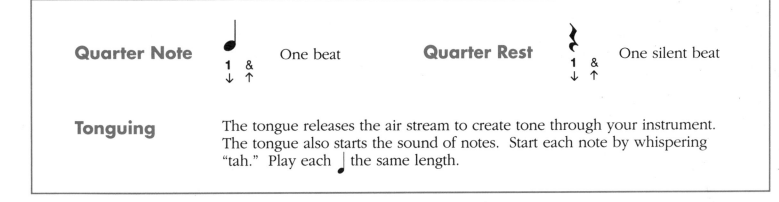

Quarter Note		One beat	Quarter Rest		One silent beat
	1 & ↓ ↑			1 & ↓ ↑	

Tonguing — The tongue releases the air stream to create tone through your instrument. The tongue also starts the sound of notes. Start each note by whispering "tah." Play each ♩ the same length.

16. PLAY TOGETHER

Before playing, count aloud and clap each ♩
Open your hands for each ⸲ Keep a steady beat.

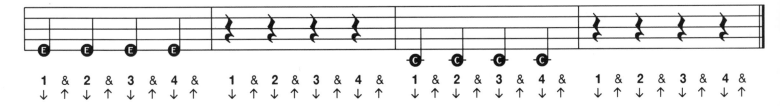

Rhythm — Rhythm is a pattern of long and short sounds played over a steady beat. Rhythm is one of the three basic elements of music, along with Melody and Harmony.

17. DOWN AND UP

Clap the rhythm before playing. Keep a steady beat.

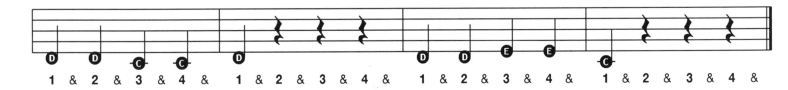

Melody — Melody is a series of notes written in a specific pattern to form a recognizable tune. Melody is one of the three basic elements of music, along with Rhythm and Harmony.

18. INSTANT SUCCESS QUIZ

What is the name of this melody?

American Folk Song

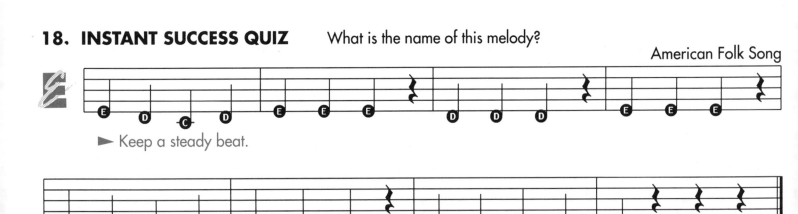

► Keep a steady beat.

Treble Clef

A **clef** is a symbol found at the beginning of each new line of music. Clefs indicate a specific set of note names. The **treble clef** appears in music written for flute, oboe, all clarinets, all saxophones, trumpet, horn, baritone t.c., bells, violin, guitar and treble voices.

Note Names

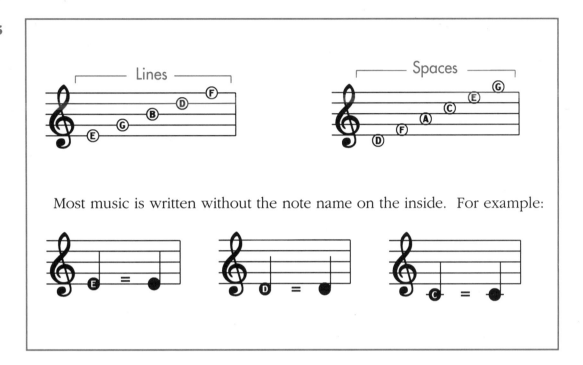

19. LET'S PLAY "F"

► "F" is placed on the bottom space of the music staff.

Breath Mark ' Take a deep breath before playing the next note.

20. MORNING DANCE   Name the notes before you play.

Slavic Folk Song

► Keep your shoulders back and relaxed.

21. A SIMPLE SONG   Count and clap the rhythm before you play. Keep a steady beat.

► Keep a steady air stream flowing through your instrument.

10

22. LET'S PLAY "G"

○ ○ ○

► "G" is placed on the second line of the music staff.

23. FIVE NOTE PATTERN

► Keep your fingers close to the instrument.

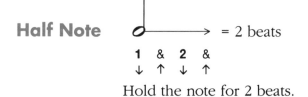

Half Note ♩ → = 2 beats

1 & 2 &
↓ ↑ ↓ ↑

Hold the note for 2 beats.

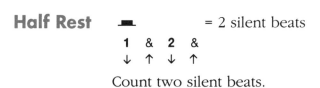

Half Rest ▬ = 2 silent beats

1 & 2 &
↓ ↑ ↓ ↑

Count two silent beats.

24. CLAP AND COUNT THE RHYTHM

Hold your hands together for 2 beats on each ♩
Open your hands on the ▬

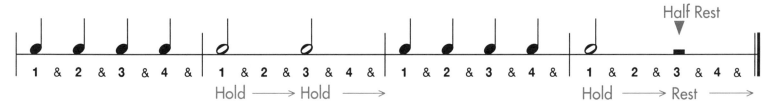

25. AT PIERROT'S DOOR

Count and clap the rhythm before you play.

French Folk Song

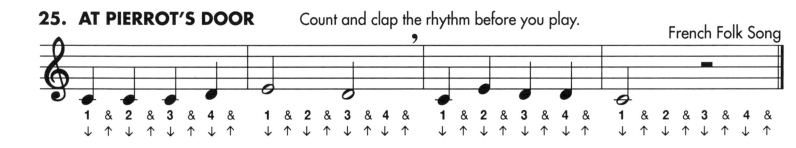

26. INSTANT SUCCESS QUIZ

Write in the note names before you play.

German Folk Song

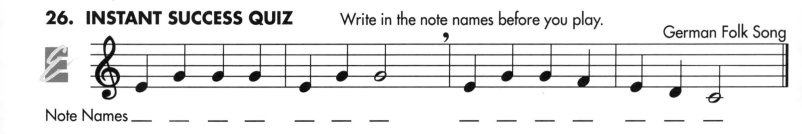

Note Names __ __ __ __ __ __ __ __ __

Time Signature (Meter)

 = 4 beats per measure

= ♩ or 𝄽 gets one beat

The time signature tells us **how many beats** are in each measure *and* **what kind of note** gets one beat. The time signature is placed next to the clef on the first line of music.

27. AURA LEE

▼ Time signature

Whole Note

𝅝 ——→ = 4 beats

1 & 2 & 3 & 4 &
↓ ↑ ↓ ↑ ↓ ↑ ↓ ↑

Hold the note for 4 beats.

Whole Rest	▬	**hangs** from the line.
Half Rest	▬	**sits** on the line.

Whole Rest

▬ = 1 silent measure

1 & 2 & 3 & 4 &
↓ ↑ ↓ ↑ ↓ ↑ ↓ ↑

Count one entire measure rest.

28. COUNT AND CLAP   Hold your hands together for 4 beats on each 𝅝

1 & 2 & 3 & 4 & | 1 & 2 & 3 & 4 & | 1 & 2 & 3 & 4 & | 1 & 2 & 3 & 4 &

Hold ————————→   Hold ————————→

29. WHOLE NOTE MARCH   Identify the time signature.

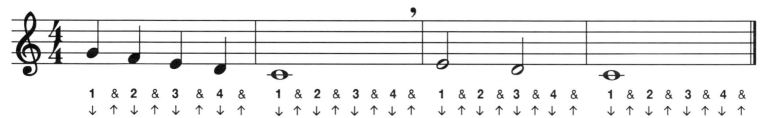

1 & 2 & 3 & 4 &   1 & 2 & 3 & 4 &   1 & 2 & 3 & 4 &   1 & 2 & 3 & 4 &
↓ ↑ ↓ ↑ ↓ ↑ ↓ ↑   ↓ ↑ ↓ ↑ ↓ ↑ ↓ ↑   ↓ ↑ ↓ ↑ ↓ ↑ ↓ ↑   ↓ ↑ ↓ ↑ ↓ ↑ ↓ ↑

30. LET'S PLAY "A"

► "A" is placed on the second space of the music staff.

31. INSTANT SUCCESS QUIZ   Name the notes before you play.

Band Performance

Band performance is one of the most rewarding opportunities you can experience. Full band arrangements and compositions are written so band members can play together. Rehearsal numbers help you find your place when practicing with other band members. Every instrument plays their own important part. Keep practicing, and you'll enjoy a lifetime of musical success!

LIGHTLY ROW - Full Band Arrangement

German Folk Song
Arr. Michael Sweeney

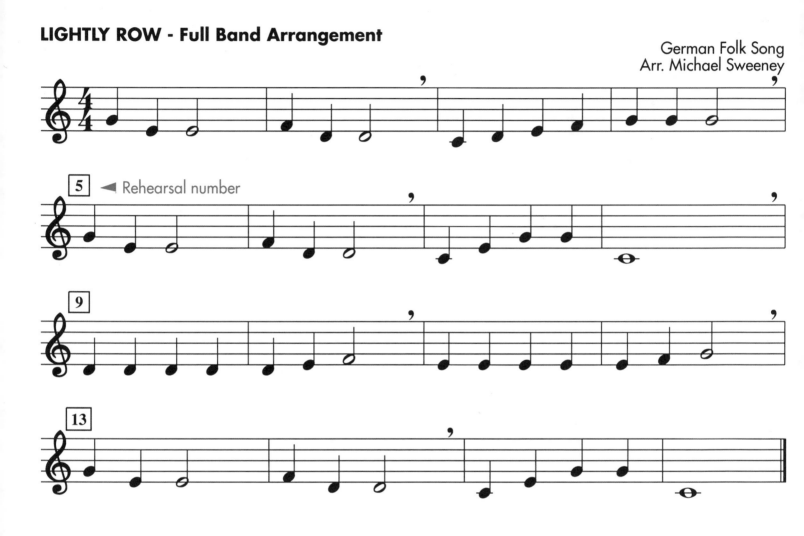

◄ Rehearsal number

Harmony

Harmony is two of more different tones sounding at the same time.
Harmony is one of the three basic elements of music, along with Rhythm and Melody.

LONDON BRIDGE - Full Band Arrangement

Arr. Michael Sweeney

OH, SUSANNA - Full Band Arrangement

American Folk Song
Arr. Michael Sweeney

Ludwig van Beethoven (1770-1827) was one of the world's greatest composers. He became completely deaf in 1802. Although he could not hear music like we do, he could "hear" it in his mind. The theme of his Symphony No. 9 is called "Ode To Joy." It was composed to the text of a poem by German writer Johann von Schiller. "Ode To Joy" was featured in concerts celebrating the reunification of Germany in 1990.

ODE TO JOY - Full Band Arrangement

Ludwig van Beethoven
Arr. Michael Sweeney

B♭ TRUMPET FINGERING CHART

B♭ Trumpet

B♭ Cornet

Instruments courtesy of
Yamaha Corporation of America
Band and Orchestral Division.

 = UP ● = PRESSED DOWN

Take Special Care

After practicing, do the following:
- Use the water key to empty water from the instrument. Blow air through the trumpet while opening the water key.
- Remove the mouthpiece. Wash your mouthpiece once per week.
- Carefully place the instrument back in the case.
- Your director will help you apply valve oil and slide grease when necessary.

F♯

G

G♯ A♭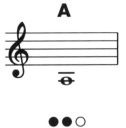

A

A♯ B♭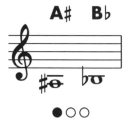

B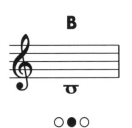

C

C♯ D♭

GLOSSARY

Term		Definition	Page
Air Stream		Produces sound through the instrument, along with your embouchure.	2
Band Performance		Playing in concert.	12
Bar Lines	𝄀	Divide the music staff into measures.	6
Basic Elements of Music		Rhythm, Melody and Harmony.	8, 9, 11
Bass Clef	𝄢	Clef used by trb., bar. b.c., bsn. tuba, timp., cello, string bass and bass voices.	9*
Beat		The pulse of music.	7
Beethoven, Ludwig van		German composer (1770-1827) who wrote "Ode To Joy."	12
Breath Mark	,	Take a deep breath before playing the next note.	9
Brass "Buzz"		Method of producing sound on brass instruments.	2*
Double Bar	𝄀	Indicates the end of the music.	8
Embouchure		Your mouth's position on the mouthpiece of the instrument.	2
Half Note	𝅗𝅥	Hold the note for 2 beats.	10
Half Rest	▬	Count 2 silent beats.	10
Harmony		Two or more different tones sounding at the same time. (Basic element)	11
Leger Lines	𝅘𝅥 , 𝅗𝅥	Extend notes above and below music staff.	7
Long Tones	○→	Best way to develop tone on your instrument.	4
Measure		A segment of music divided by bar lines.	6
Melody		Series of notes written in a specific pattern to form a recognizable tune. (Basic element)	8
Meter		Tells how many beats are in each measure *and* what kind of note gets one beat.	11
Mouthpiece Work-Outs		Method of checking embouchure.	2
Music Staff		Lines and spaces where notes are placed.	6
Note Names			9*
Notes	𝅘𝅥 , 𝅗𝅥 , 𝅝	Tells how high or low to play *and* how long to play.	6
Posture		How you sit when playing your instrument.	3
Practicing		A necessary part of learning to play an instrument. Set weekly goals and plan accordingly.	inside front cover
Quarter Note	𝅘𝅥	Play for one beat.	7
Quarter Rest	𝄽	Count one silent beat.	7
Rhythm		Pattern of long and short sounds played over the beat. (Basic element)	9
Stem		Thin line placed on the right 𝅘𝅥 or left 𝅘𝅥 of notes.	6
Time Signature (Meter)		Tells how many beats are in each measure *and* what kind of note gets one beat.	11
Tone		Musical sound.	2
Tonguing		Releases your air stream and starts notes.	8
Treble Clef	𝄞	Clef used by fl., ob., all clars., all saxes, tpt., horn, bar. t.c., bells, guitar, vln., and treble voices.	9*
Whole Note	𝅝	Hold the note for 4 beats.	11
Whole Rest	▬	Count one full measure rest.	11

* Term only appears in corresponding instrument book.